DISCARD

THE ART OF WAR

from SmarterComics

SUN TZU

D1280457

Shane Clester	Pencils and Inks
Mike Oliveri	Editor
Cullen Bunn	Script
Tony Fleecs	Cover design
Steward Doering	Colors
Sander Pieterse	Creative director
Franco Arda	CEO SmarterComics

Printed in Canada

Copyright © 2011 by SmarterComics.

ISBN: 978-1-61082-008-0

Published by SmarterComics LLC, 111 N. Market Street, Suite 300, San Jose, CA 95113
Phone: 408 786 5444, www.smartercomics.com.

All rights reserved.

This book is based on Sun Tzu's The Art of War, translated by Lionel Giles, M.A. (1910).

INTRODUCTION

Originally inscribed on bamboo strips about 500 B.C., **THE ART OF WAR is among the oldest books ever written.** It is also one of the most successful books on military strategy ever conceived, and it is still used today by the military, including the U.S. Marine Corps. But its influence has stretched far beyond the military. Sun Tzu's philosophies have been quoted in countless books and movies and taught in business schools. Film makers, athletes, lawyers, negotiators, investors, and even gang members quote from the work.

Don't let the book title fool you—THE ART OF WAR is less about war than about the art of winning. Conflict arises for all of us, whether in business, sports, politics, or personal life. Sun Tzu's goal for THE ART OF WAR was to describe the best way to prevent conflicts in the first place—to outsmart an opponent so that physical battle is not necessary. A general with a reputation for invincibility, Sun Tzu taught strategies for prevailing as quickly as possible against an opponent—with minimal loss of life and property. Every aphorism explained by Sun Tzu (including taking calculated risks and thinking thoroughly before acting) represents a tactic that, when wisely applied, **can generate a winning strategy in many areas of daily life.**

A warning: this (comic) book is deceptive. **It is short enough to be read in 60 minutes, but subtle enough to be studied for years—even for a lifetime.** Many people have tried to reach into Sun Tzu's book only to find the ancient text too difficult to read. SmarterComics believes this classic should be accessible to a wide audience. That's why we tried something new: modifying the original transla¬tion for ease of understanding and to conform to a comic book format. In order to make it most relevant and understandable, we present Sun Tzu's philosophy with illustrated scenes from the 21st century.

It sounds paradoxical, but **by better understanding conflict, we might actually prevent conflict and contribute to a more peaceful society.**

Your SmarterComics team

CHICAGO

1927

DON CUMMUTA AND HIS MEN HAVE A FIRM GRIP ON THE CITY'S CRIME RACKETS, BUT THAT GRIP IS STARTING TO SLIP AS RIVAL GROUPS MUSCLE IN ON HIS TURF, AND HE KNOWS HE CAN'T JUST BACK DOWN.

THE DON IS NO STRANGER TO BLOODSHED,
AND HIS MEN ARE WILLING AND ABLE TO FIGHT.

YET THE COSTS OF VIOLENCE ARE GREAT,
AND HE WILL HAVE TO EXAMINE THEM
CLOSELY BEFORE ISSUING ORDERS.

IS VIOLENCE THE ONLY ANSWER?
OR WILL THE DON FIND A WAY TO WIN HIS
BATTLES WITHOUT DIRECT CONFLICT?

IF YOU'RE GOING TO FIGHT, DON CUMMUTA, YOU MUST FIRST COUNT THE COST.

ANYONE CAN GO TO BATTLE, BUT THE HEIGHT OF WISDOM IS TO WIN WITHOUT A BATTLE

HOW SO?

WAR IS COSTLY. EVEN IF YOU WIN, YOU LOSE. WAR COSTS LIVES, ENERGY, MONEY, AND TIME.

HOW MUCH ARE YOU PREPARED TO LOSE?

BUT I GOTTA DO SOMETHIN' ABOUT THESE MOOKS CROWDIN' IN ON MY RACKET!

IT'S NOT A QUESTION OF INACTION.

YOUR GOAL SHOULD NOT BE TO WIN BATTLES, BUT TO PREVENT THEM WHENEVER POSSIBLE.

HMMM...

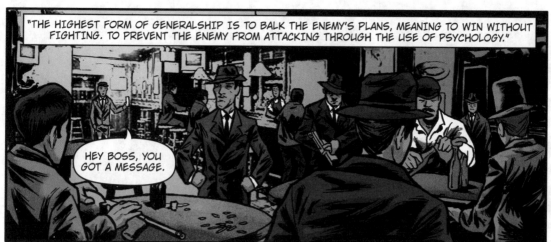

"THE HIGHEST FORM OF GENERALSHIP IS TO BALK THE ENEMY'S PLANS, MEANING TO WIN WITHOUT FIGHTING. TO PREVENT THE ENEMY FROM ATTACKING THROUGH THE USE OF PSYCHOLOGY."

HEY BOSS, YOU GOT A MESSAGE.

CUMMUTA WANTS TO HAVE A SIT-DOWN.

LATER...

UH...MAYBE WE COULD WORK SOMETHIN' OUT.

PREVENT THE JUNCTION OF THE ENEMY'S FORCES. IN OTHER WORDS, NEGOTIATE WITH HIM. SIT DOWN WITH THE ENEMY AND FIND A PEACEFUL SOLUTION.

I THINK THAT'D BE A MOST BENEFICIAL IDEA.

WASHINGTON, D.C.
1993

HOTSHOT YOUNG LAWYER TIM HENDRICKS HAS
HIS EYE ON A CONGRESSIONAL SEAT, AND THE
RE-ELECTION OF LONGTIME SENATOR IRWIN
BROWN IS THE PERFECT OPPORTUNITY.

HENDRICKS KNOWS A LONG, DRAWN-OUT CAMPAIGN SPELLS DEATH IN THE POLITICAL ARENA, AND NO MATTER WHAT THE POLLS SAY, NO ELECTION IS GUARANTEED.

WHAT HENDRICKS NEEDS IS A QUICK AND DECISIVE VICTORY.

A WAY TO WIN BEFORE HE EVEN GOES TO BATTLE ON ELECTION DAY.

SUN TZU

THERE IS NO INSTANCE OF A COUNTRY HAVING BENEFITED FROM PROLONGED WAR.

SENATE RACE — LIVE — 2:38 PT

MY GUESTS TONIGHT ARE IN A CONTENTIOUS RACE THAT RECENT POLLS INDICATE COULD GO EITHER WAY.

IF GOING TO BATTLE IS INEVITABLE, THE GOAL IS TO ACHIEVE A QUICK AND DECISIVE VICTORY.

IT'S SIMPLE, BOB. I THINK THE PEOPLE ARE READY FOR A CHANGE!

AS THE CHALLENGER, HOW DO YOU EXPECT TO GAIN GROUND ON THE INCUMBENT SENATOR?

CHANGE FOR CHANGE'S SAKE IS NO SOLUTION.

SENATE RACE

THE ART OF WAR IS NOT ABOUT AVOIDING BATTLE, BUT ABOUT PREVENTING CONFLICT BEFORE IT ARISES, AND WINNING QUICKLY AND WITH MINIMAL LOSS IF WAR IS IMMINENT.

NOR IS TREADING THE SAME PATH OVER AND OVER. WE ALL KNOW THE DEFINITION OF "CRAZY", RIGHT? OUR SUCCESSFUL CAMPAIGN FUNDRAISER SHOWS PEOPLE ARE VOTING WITH THEIR WALLETS!

MONEY DOESN'T SOLVE PROBLEMS, EITHER. PEOPLE *RESPECT* THE VALUE OF MY EXPERIENCE.

I GUESS WE'LL FIND OUT IN THE ELECTION. THANK YOU, GENTLEMEN.

WHAT HIGHER WISDOM COULD THERE BE THAN PREVENTING THE COST OF WAR BY WINNING WITHOUT FIGHTING?

THE POLLS ARE PUTTING US AHEAD BY 30 PERCENT!

EXCELLENT! I KNEW THE PEOPLE WOULD RESPOND TO OUR MESSAGE!

GENERALS WHO WIN WITHOUT GOING TO BATTLE ARE OFTEN SO PREPARED THAT THEY AVOID CONFLICT THROUGH INTIMIDATION.

THAT'S IT! I'M DROPPING OUT OF THE RACE! I CAN'T COMPETE WITH THAT!

SLAM

NEW YORK

2012

WE OFTEN THINK OF GAMING AS A MEANINGLESS LEISURE ACTIVITY, BUT IN OUR HEADS AND IN OUR HEARTS THE CONFLICTS CAN BE VERY REAL.

EMOTIONAL RESPONSES RUN HIGH, AND WHILE WE'RE ALL TAUGHT WINNING ISN'T EVERYTHING, WE ALL KNOW WINNING IS A LOT MORE FUN THAN LOSING.

RECOGNIZING THESE EMOTIONAL RESPONSES—THE NEGATIVE RESPONSES IN PARTICULAR—IS CRITICAL TO SUCCESS.

LET'S LOOK AT HOW THIS YOUNG GAMER LEARNS TO CONTROL HIS EMOTIONAL RESPONSE DURING BATTLE SO HE CAN ENJOY THE REWARD LATER.

SET ANGER ASIDE AND REACT WITH WISDOM.

−1500PTS

KEEP YOURSELF SOUND OF SPIRIT AND SOLID IN PERSPECTIVE.

@#%$#!!

IT IS THROUGH YOUR BATTLES WITH OTHERS THAT YOU WILL DISCOVER WHAT DOESN'T WORK...

...WHAT DOES WORK...

...AND HOW TO BEST PROTECT YOURSELF.

+500PTS +500PTS +500PTS

IN A WORLD WHERE PEOPLE MAKE UNEDUCATED DECISIONS, STRATEGIC WISDOM WILL HELP YOU TO RISE ABOVE YOUR OPPONENTS.

TUNISIA
1943

AN EXPEDITION MAKES ITS WAY THROUGH THE DESERT. THE INTENSE HEAT AND SCARCITY OF WATER MAKES TRAVEL DIFFICULT, AND THE SPREAD OF WORLD WAR II HAS ADDED A NEW ELEMENT OF DANGER.

THIS IS NOT A TIME
FOR RASH DECISION.

THE TROOP LEADER IS GOING TO
NEED INFORMATION AND PLANNING
IF HIS PEOPLE ARE GOING TO GET
THROUGH THE DESERT ALIVE.

*WITH NO LEADERSHIP AND NO
STRATEGY, THE GROUP IS ONLY
GAMBLING ON SUCCESS.*

ALL MEN CAN SEE THE TACTICS WHEREBY I CONQUER, BUT WHAT NONE CAN SEE IS THE STRATEGY OUT OF WHICH VICTORY IS EVOLVED.

I GET IT. IF WE CAN'T FIND PROVISIONS, WE WON'T EVEN MAKE IT TO THE BATTLE.

WE ARE OUT OF WATER!

WE'LL NEVER MAKE IT ANOTHER THREE DAYS!

WITHOUT STRATEGY, SUCCESS IS A MERE GAMBLE.

WE'RE BETTER OFF ON OUR OWN!

WAIT! WAIT!

WE NEED TO STAY TOGETHER! WE CAN SOLVE THIS PROLBEM IF WE THINK IT THROUGH!

OUR SCOUTS HAVE FOUND A TRAIL THROUGH THE CANYON.

WITH STRATEGY, WE HAVE A MAP...

...A ROUTE...

THIS PATH TAKES US THROUGHT THE MOUNTAIN PASS!

...AND A DESTINATION.

THIS LEADS US TO AN OASIS! FRESH WATER FOR EVERYONE!

THIS PATH CAN BE DANGEROUS, BUT IF WE STICK TO THE MAP, WE'LL BE ALL RIGHT!

SOON...

WE MADE IT!

WHOO HOO!

YEAH!

WE'RE SAVED!

16

PALO ALTO

2005

DR. TRENT MILLER IS A TOP SURGEON WHO HAS SAVED SCORES OF LIVES. HIS SKILLS ARE RECOGNIZED NATIONWIDE, PUTTING HIM IN HIGH DEMAND FOR SOME OF THE TOUGHEST CASES.

THERE ARE NO HALF MEASURES
IN DR. MILLER'S WORK.

AN ERROR IN JUDGEMENT OR
A MISCALCULATION DURING
DIAGNOSIS CAN RESULT IN THE
DEATH OF A PATIENT.

AS WE WILL SEE, ALL THE
REAL WORK COMES BEFORE
HE EVEN PICKS UP A SCALPEL.

THE GENERAL WHO WINS A BATTLE MAKES MANY CALCULATIONS IN HIS TEMPLE BEFORE THE BATTLE IS FOUGHT.

HERE ARE MR DONOVAN'S X-RAYS, DR. MILLER.

AS LIFE PRESENTS YOU WITH CONFLICT, FIND A SOLITARY PLACE WHERE YOU CAN FIND BALANCE.

THIS IS WORSE THAN I FEARED.

THINK THOROUGHLY BEFORE YOU ACT.

CALCULATE THE COST OF CONFRONTATION BEFORE YOU RUSH INTO BATTLE.

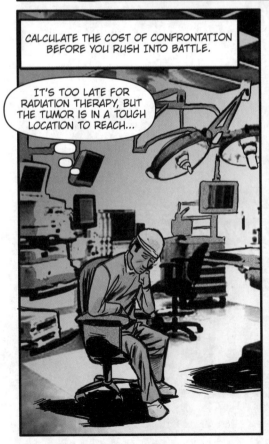

IT'S TOO LATE FOR RADIATION THERAPY, BUT THE TUMOR IS IN A TOUGH LOCATION TO REACH...

THE SURGERY IS RISKY, BUT I THINK IT'S OUR BEST CHANCE OF SAVING YOUR LIVE.

LET'S DO IT.

BEFORE YOU COMMIT YOURSELF TO WAR, YOU MUST MAKE SURE IT IS THE ONLY OPTION.

IF YOU COMMIT TO BATTLE, COMMIT FULLY.

HALF AN EFFORT CAN RESULT IN DEFEAT.

AVOID SETTLING FOR A QUICK SOLUTION.

ALRIGHT, I THINK THAT'S GOT IT.

TAKING THE TIME TO NOT JUST DO WHAT IS EASY, BUT WHAT IS RIGHT WILL DETERMINE THE LONGEVITY OF YOUR SUCCESS.

I FEEL GREAT! THE DOCTOR REALLY DID A GREAT JOB!

THE AMAZON
1954

TREASURE HUNTING IS A DANGEROUS GAME,
BUT FOR MEN LIKE CHARLIE FUCHS AND
GUNNAR WOLFE, THE PROMISE OF FAME AND
FORTUNE IS WELL WORTH THE RISK.

RISK IS A PART OF EVERY VENTURE. NO OUTCOME IS GUARANTEED.

THE KEY IS ANALYZING THE RISK AND HAVING THE COURAGE TO ACT ON IT.

FUCHS AND WOLFE ARE ABOUT TO LEARN THE COMPLEX RELATIONSHIP BETWEEN COURAGE AND RISK.

COWARDICE LEADS TO CAPTURE.

DID YOU HEAR SOMETHING?

EVERY MOVE WE MAKE REQUIRES RISK.

HEADHUNTERS!

I CAN'T GO ON.

I'M STAYING HERE.

DOING NOTHING IS ALSO A RISK.

THE GREATEST RISK COULD BE ATTEMPTING TO UPHOLD THE STATUS QUO.

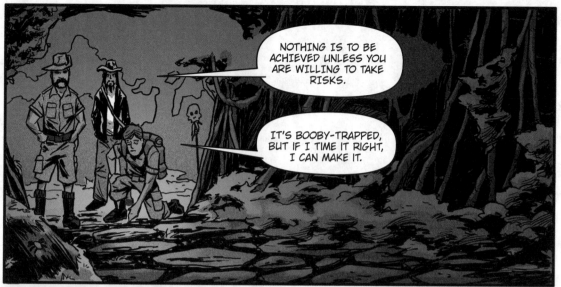

NOTHING IS TO BE ACHIEVED UNLESS YOU ARE WILLING TO TAKE RISKS.

IT'S BOOBY-TRAPPED, BUT IF I TIME IT RIGHT, I CAN MAKE IT.

WHOO

PFFT

WHOOSH

PFFT

COURAGE IS BIRTHED BY CONFIDENCE; ACTING IN AN EFFORT TO DO THE RIGHT THING.

AT THE OTHER END OF THE SPECTRUM, OVERCONFIDENCE CAN BE DANGEROUS.

PIECE OF CAKE!

THOK

URK!

BUT OF COURSE, BRAVERY WITHOUT FORETHOUGHT LEADS TO RECKLESSNESS.

LOS ANGELES
1982

THE SWAT TEAM FACES A VARIETY OF
THREATS, RANGING FROM TERRORISTS AND
SEPARATIST GROUPS TO DRUG DEALERS AND
BANK ROBBERS.

THEY ARE THE ELITE OF LAW ENFORCEMENT
UNITS, OFTEN RECEIVING THE BEST
EQUIPMENT AND THE BEST TRAINING.

HOWEVER, NOT
EVEN THE SWAT
TEAM CHARGES
INTO EVERY
CONFLICT WITH
GUNS BLAZING.

THEY MUST CONSIDER EACH
SITUATION AND DETERMINE WHEN
TO FIGHT AND WHEN TO WAIT.

WITH A TEN TO ONE ADVANTAGE, YOUR OVERWHELMING STRENGTH CAN BE DISPLAYED IN SUCH A WAY THAT SURRENDER IS YOUR ENEMY'S ONLY OPTION.

THE PIGS DON'T THINK I'M SERIOUS? I'LL BLOW US ALL UP!

JUST TRY ME.

1. IF YOUR FORCES ARE TEN TO THE ENEMY'S ONE, SURROUND HIM.

AH, CRAP.

NOT ONLY WILL THIS APPROACH YIELD THE GREATEST VICTORY— ONE THAT REQUIRES NO BLOODSHED—IT CAN ALSO RESULT IN THE RESPECT, ADMIRATION AND TRUST OF YOU OPPONENT.

WHEN THE ODDS ARE EVEN, SUN TZU DECLARES THAT BATTLE CAN BE OFFERED. HE DOES NOT RECOMMEND YOU FIGHT.

PREPARE TO BREACH.

IF FORCED TO, YOU MUST BE ABLE TO DEFEND YOURSELF. IN THIS CASE NOT TO WIN, BUT TO SURVIVE.

BOOM

2. IF FIVE TO ONE, ATTACK HIM.

POLICE! SHOW ME YOUR HANDS!

3. IF TWICE AS NUMEROUS, DIVIDE YOUR ARMY IN TWO.

ALPHA TEAM HAS SECURED THE EXITS.

BRAVO TEAM BREACH IN 3... 2... 1...

GO GO GO!

HOLD YOUR HEAD HIGH IF AFTER CAREFUL CONTEMPLATION, YOU DECIDE NOT TO BATTLE TO AVERT DEFEAT.

ANY MOVE YOU MAKE, MAKE IT ONLY IF IT WILL BENEFIT YOUR STRATEGY. OTHERWISE USE YOUR ENERGY TO STRENGTHEN YOURSELF AND IMPROVE YOUR POSITION.

BROOKLYN

1963

JOHNNY MORGAN IS AN INNOCENT MAN,
SENTENCED TO LIFE IN PRISON FOR THE
MURDER OF A HIGH-PROFILE CELEBRITY. THE
CASE MADE ALL THE PAPERS AND PUBLIC
OPINION BURIED HIM BEFORE THE GAVEL FELL,
MAKING IT A TOUGH CASE FOR ANY LAWYER TO
HANDLE.

PROCLAIMING ONE'S INNOCENCE IS ONE THING, BUT PROVING IT TO A JUDGE AND JURY IS ANOTHER MATTER ENTIRELY.

WITH THE WEIGHT OF THE LEGAL SYSTEM COMING DOWN UPON THEM, AND THE PUBLIC SCRUTINY THE APPEAL WILL GENERATE, MORGAN'S LAWYERS WILL HAVE TO MOVE FORWARD WITH GREAT CARE.

WITHOUT CAREFUL PREPARATION, THEY PUT BOTH THEIR CLIENT AND THEIR OWN REPUTATIONS AT RISK.

HE WILL WIN WHO KNOWS WHEN TO FIGHT AND WHEN NOT TO FIGHT.

DO YOU THINK WE SHOULD TAKE THIS TO TRIAL?

THERE IS NO CLEAR PRECEDENT HERE. WE'RE GOING TO HAVE TO DO OUR HOMEWORK.

CAUTION DOES NOT PREVENT YOU FROM KNOWING WHEN—OR WHEN NOT TO—WAGE WAR; ARROGANCE DOES.

THIS MAY BE JUST WHAT WE NEED...

TO AVOID MAKING DECISIONS BASED ON ARROGANCE, YOU MUST SECLUDE YOURSELF TO A QUIET PLACE AND CONSIDER YOUR SITUATION.

PAINTING A PICTURE IN YOUR MIND OF THE CONSEQUENCES OF YOUR DECISION—BEFORE MAKING THAT DECISION—WILL HELP YOU TO KNOW WHEN YOU CAN FIGHT AND WIN AND WHEN YOU WILL BE UNABLE.

HE WILL WIN WHO KNOWS HOW TO HANDLE BOTH SUPERIOR AND INFERIOR FORCES.

THE STATE SEES THIS APPEAL AS A FRIVOLOUS WASTE OF TIME AND RESOURCES, YOUR HONOR.

HE WILL WIN WHOSE ARMY IS ANIMATED BY THE SAME SPIRIT THROUGHOUT ALL ITS RANKS.

THIS IS BRILLIANT! I CAN'T BELIEVE WE DIDN'T THINK OF IT EARLIER!

HE WILL WIN WHO, PREPARED HIMSELF, WAITS TO TAKE THE ENEMY UNPREPARED.

YOUR HONOR, THE DEFENSE HAS LEARNED THE DETECTIVE WAS FACING SUSPENSION. AT THE TIME OF ARREST.

WE FEEL HE MANIPULATED THE CASE FOR A QUICK ARREST FOR PERSONAL GAIN. OUR EVIDENCE HAS BEEN PRESENTED.

HE WILL WIN WHO HAS MILITARY CAPACITY AND IS NOT INTERFERED WITH BY THE RULER OF THE LAND.

VERY WELL. THE COURT WILL HEAR THE APPEAL AT 9AM TOMORROW MORNING.

WE DID IT!

PARIS
1988

HENRI BROUSSEAU IS A FENCER HUNGRY FOR HIS FIRST WORLD CHAMPIONSHIP. IT'S BEEN A TOUGH TOURNAMENT, AND HE'S ABOUT TO GO UP AGAINST THREE-TIME CHAMPION MATHIEU MARCHAND IN THE TITLE MATCH.

HENRI KNOWS PREPARATION IS KEY.

HE HAS STUDIED HIS
OPPONENT WITH GREAT CARE.

YET IS THAT ENOUGH? HAS
HE REMEMBERED TO LOOK
INWARD AS WELL?

KNOWING YOUR OPPONENT ENABLES YOU TO TAKE THE OFFENSIVE. KNOWING YOURSELF ENABLES YOU TO STAND ON THE DEFENSIVE.

IDENTIFY YOUR STRENGTHS AND WEAKNESSES. WITH THIS KNOWLEDGE, BUILD YOUR DEFENSE.

WHILE KNOWING YOURSELF IS THE KEY TO SUCCESS, KNOW YOURSELF ACCURATELY TO ENSURE SUCCESS.

I'VE STUDIED TAPES OF HIS MATCHES. I'M READY FOR THIS.

NOT KNOWING YOUR ENEMY EQUATES TO GAMBLING AND REDUCES YOUR CHANCES OF WINNING TO ONLY HALF.

EN GARDE!

POINT!

IF YOU KNOW NEITHER THE ENEMY NOR YOUR-SELF, YOU WILL SUCCUMB IN EVERY BATTLE.

IF YOU KNOW YOURSELF BUT NOT THE ENEMY, FOR EVERY VICTORY GAINED YOU WILL ALSO SUFFER DEFEAT.

KNOWING YOURSELF WILL AID IN YOUR ATTACK, BUT NOT IN YOUR DEFENSE.

IF YOU KNOW THE ENEMY AND KNOW YOURSELF, YOU NEED NOT FEAR THE RESULT OF A HUNDRED BATTLES.

POINT!

KNOWING THE ENEMY WILL ENABLE YOU TO DEFEND YOURSELF. KNOWING YOURSELF WILL ENABLE YOU TO ATTACK.

ATTACK.

POINT!

POINT! WINNER!

LAS VEGAS
2009

THE POKER CHAMPIONSHIPS ARE HIGH STAKES
TOURNAMENTS, OFTEN WITH MILLIONS OF
DOLLARS AT STAKE. ONLY A NOVICE BELIEVES
POKER IS A GAME OF CHANCE.

POKER IS A BATTLE OF WILLS.

IT'S NOT ALWAYS THE CARDS IN A PLAYER'S HAND
THAT DETERMINE THE OUTCOME, BUT THE CARDS
THE OPPONENT BELIEVES THE PLAYER HOLDS.

THE BEST PLAYERS KNOW
TO BALANCE DECEPTION
WITH A DEMONSTRATION
OF STRENGTH.

ALL WARFARE IS BASED ON DECEPTION.

WORLD POKER CHAMPIONSHIP

FOR EXAMPLE, THE BLUFF.

EVEN WHEN WE ARE ABLE TO ATTACK, WE MUST SEEM UNABLE.

DRAW YOUR ENEMY IN WITH THE PROSPECT TO GAIN, THEN TAKE THEM BY CONFUSION.

RAISE.

SCENARIO 1: LURE YOUR ENEMY INTO NOT ATTACKING YOU. SCENARIO 2: MAKE YOURSELF APPARENT, INVITING THE ENEMY TO ATTACK YOU.

WHICH OF THESE SCENARIOS IS MORE HUMANE? THE ANSWER IS ACTUALLY THE FIRST.

I FOLD.

THE MASTER OF WAR PUTS HIMSELF BEYOUND THE POSSIBILITY OF DEFEAT, AND THEN WAITS FOR AN OPPORTUNITY TO DEFEAT THE ENEMY.

NEVER UNDERESTIMATE YOUR OPPONENT'S STRENGTH.

IF YOU DO NOT HAVE THE ADVANTAGE OF STRENGTH, THEN PAUSE.

I'M ALL IN.

IF YOU DO, THEN TAKE ACTION.

FOUR -OF-A-KIND.

THE HAND WINS THE POT, AND THE PLAYER WINS THE TOURNAMENT.

CONGRATULATIONS!

ST. LOUIS
1991

BRAD CLARK IS TIRED OF LABORING AWAY IN A
DEAD-END JOB WITH A PITTANCE SALARY. HE
KNOWS HE CAN DO BETTER.

BRAD HAS A GREAT IDEA FOR A STORE ALL HIS OWN, A STORE HE THINKS CAN BE VERY SUCCESSFUL.

YET THE IDEA ITSELF IS JUST THE BEGINNING, ESPECIALLY IN A MARKET DOMINATED BY BIG BOX SUPERSTORES AND ONLINE RETAILERS.

BRAD WILL LEARN HE NEEDS TO PICK HIS BATTLES CAREFULLY AND STRIKE WHEN THE TIME IS RIGHT.

ENERGY MAY BE LIKENED TO THE BENDING OF A BOW.

DECISION MAY BE LIKENED TO LOOSING THE ARROW.

IT'S BEEN A PLEASURE WORKING WITH YOU,

BUT I THINK IT'S HIGH TIME I SET OUT ON MY OWN.

TIMING IS EVERYTHING.

THIS PLACE LOOKS PROMISING. I'LL GIVE THEM A CALL.

FOR LEASE

503-368-3738

SO... I JUST DECIDED THAT I NEEDED TO OPEN MY OWN SWEATER BOUTIQUE!

BUT...DIDN'T YOU HEAR ABOUT THAT SWEATER SUPERSTORE THAT JUST OPENED UP?

SUPERSTORE?

HOW CAN I COMPETE WITH THAT?

IF THE COMPETITION IS SUPERIOR IN STRENGTH, EVADE HIM.

OTHERWISE ATTACK HIM WHERE HE IS UNPREPARED. APPEAR WHERE YOU ARE NOT EXPECTED.

NOW MORE COLORS

BLUE! GREEN! YELLOW! PURPLE! MAGENTA!

NEW! COLORS!

EVERY COLOR!!

APPEAR WHERE YOU ARE NOT EXPECTED.

GRAND OPENING
ALL-BLACK SWEATERS

I BET THEY NEVER SAW THIS COMING!

HIP & COOL!!

CHOOSE YOUR BATTLES CAREFULLY. THE GREATEST ADVANTAGE IS WHEN YOUR OPPONENT DOESN'T KNOW THEY HAVE BEEN SURPRISED AT ALL.

DETROIT
1985

MC REILLY J IS A TALENTED STREET POET, A RAPPER WITH A LOT OF SKILL AND AMBITION STUCK LOW ON THE FOOD CHAIN BELOW THE LABEL'S FAVORED SON, BROTHER FLEX.

HIS FRIENDS TELL HIM HE SHOULD WALK AWAY, THAT HE'LL NEVER GET ANYWHERE BY CONTINUING TO MAKE BROTHER FLEX LOOK GOOD.

FORTUNATELY MC REILLY J IS PATIENT. HE KNOWS THERE IS OPPORTUNITY IN WORKING WITH THE LABEL.

AND HE HAS THE SENSE TO STRIKE WHEN THAT OPPORTUNITY RISES. AND HE HAS THE SENSE TO STRIKE WHEN THAT OPPORTUNITY RISES.

THE GOOD FIGHTERS OF OLD FIRST PUT THEMSELVES BEYOND THE POSSIBILITY OF DEFEAT...

MAYBE YOU SHOULDN'T DRINK SO MUCH BEFORE WE CUT THAT NEW TRACK.

DON'T TELL ME WHAT TO DO!

I'M THE BEST RAPPER ON THE LABEL. IF I DON'T CUT THE TRACK, WHO ELSE ARE THEY GONNA GET?

PREPARATION LEADS TO INVINCIBILITY.

WHY NOT ME? WAIT 'TIL I SHOW THEM THESE RHYMES!

YOU?

THE GOOD FIGHTER WAITS FOR AN OPPORTUNITY TO DEFEAT THE ENEMY.

YOU'RE READY FOR THIS. YOU CAN AFFORD TO WAIT PATIENTLY UNTIL HE SHOWS YOU A WEAKNESS.

WHEN THE VULNERABILITY BECOMES APPARENT...

...STRIKE WITH FORCE!

WHAT'S WRONG WITH YOU?

ON AIR

ARE YOU DRUNK AGAIN? THAT'S IT! YOU'RE GOING TO REHAB!

PREPARATION PROTECTS YOU AND PROVIDES THE SPACE YOU NEED TO FIND THE PERFECT MOMENT TO ATTACK.

HOW ARE WE GOING TO FINISH THE ALBUM NOW?

UHHH... I CAN RAP.

DENVER
1979

DETECTIVE TIM MANGAN IS A VETERAN
HOMICIDE DETECTIVE WHO'S SEEN IT ALL. HE
KNOWS WHEN HE'S GOT HIS MAN, BUT HE
ALSO KNOWS HE CAN'T GET A CONVICTION ON
GUT FEELING.

THE ABILITY TO READ A SUSPECT IS ONE OF THE MOST IMPORTANT WEAPONS IN MANGAN'S ARSENAL.

HE NEEDS TO EXAMINE THE SUSPECT'S STRENGTHS AND WEAKNESSES, AND FIND OUT WHAT THE SUSPECT MAY BE HIDING.

ONCE THE SUSPECT REVEALS HIMSELF, MANGAN STRIKES.

FORCE YOUR ENEMY TO REVEAL HIMSELF, SO AS TO FIND HIS VULNERABLE SPOTS.

LET'S GO OVER THIS ONE MORE TIME...

YOU SAY YOU'VE NEVER SEEN THE VICTIM BEFORE...THAT YOU DON'T KNOW ANYTHING ABOUT THE MURDER...

WATCH HOW DETECTIVE MANGAN WORKS THE SUSPECT.

BY BAITING HIM AND OBSERVING HIS REACTIONS, THE DETECTIVE WILL FIND THE SUSPECT'S STRENGTHS AND WEAKNESSES.

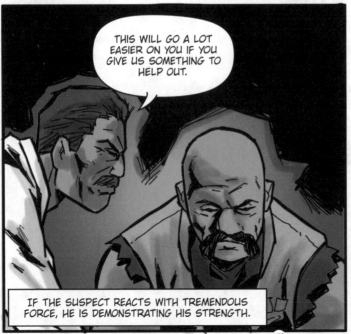

THIS WILL GO A LOT EASIER ON YOU IF YOU GIVE US SOMETHING TO HELP OUT.

IF THE SUSPECT REACTS WITH TREMENDOUS FORCE, HE IS DEMONSTRATING HIS STRENGTH.

I ALREADY TOLD YOU, I DON'T KNOW A THING! I WANT MY LAWYER!

FAIR ENOUGH. IT MAY TAKE A WHILE, SO YOU MAY AS WELL MAKE YOURSELF COMFORTABLE.

HOW ARE WE GOING TO PLAY THIS?

WHATEVER WE DO, WE BETTER MAKE IT QUICK. AS SOON AS HIS LAWYER GETS HERE, HE'S GOING TO WALK.

I'VE GOT AN IDEA. JUST WAIT HERE FOR A SECOND.

WE'VE PUT A CALL IN TO YOUR ATTORNEY.

JUST SO YOU KNOW, WE'VE GOT A WITNESS IN THE NEXT ROOM WHO PUTS YOU AND YOUR BIKE AT THE SCENE.

IF THE SUSPECT TESTS THE WATERS, THEN HE IS LIKELY TO BE HIDING A WEAKNESS.

WAIT A MINUTE... WHAT?

UH, WHAT KIND OF DEAL ARE YOU OFFERING?

WICHITA

2007

SAM DONNELLY IS ABOUT TO GIVE AN
IMPORTANT LESSON IN WARFARE TO HIS
COWORKERS AT THE ANNUAL COMPANY
PAINTBALL MATCH.

HIS ENTIRE TEAM HAS BEEN TAKEN OUT, LEAVING HIM TO DEFEND THE IT DEPARTMENT'S CHAMPIONSHIP.

HE COULD SURRENDER, LET THE OTHER TEAM FINISH HIM OFF SO HE COULD GO HAVE A BEER AND A BURGER.

OR HE COULD INTRODUCE THE OTHER TEAM TO THE CONCEPT OF FORMLESSNESS AND BRING THE CHAMPIONSHIP TROPHY HOME ALONE.

THOUGH THE ENEMY MAY BE STRONGER IN NUMBER, WE CAN STILL PREVENT HIM FROM WINNING.

ONLY ONE PLAYER STANDING ON THE BLUE TEAM!

A WEAKER ARMY CAN DEFEAT A STRONGER ONE THROUGH FORMLESSNESS.

THOUGH THE PLAYER IS ALONE, HE CAN BE FAST AND NIMBLE.

HE'S AROUND HERE SOMEWHERE...

FORMLESSNESS GIVES ONE TREMENDOUS FLEXIBILITY WITHOUT REDUCING POWER.

WHERE IS HE? HOW MANY ARE LEFT—

WITH FORMLESSNESS, ONE CAN ATTACK A MULTITUDE OF WEAKNESSES SIMULTANEOUSLY...

...WHICH GIVES THE APPEARANCE OF HAVING A FAR LARGER FORCE THAN ONE ACTUALLY BRINGS.

ACK!

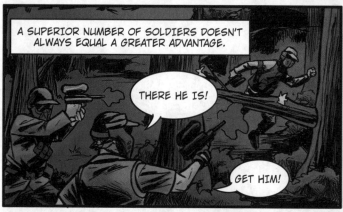

A SUPERIOR NUMBER OF SOLDIERS DOESN'T ALWAYS EQUAL A GREATER ADVANTAGE.

THERE HE IS!

GET HIM!

HE WHO BEST UTILIZES RESOURCES WILL FIND THE ADVANTAGE.

WHERE'D HE GO?

THE BLUE TEAM WINS!

SEATTLE
1999

VETERAN WRESTLER ERIC VON MIDGARD IS
TRYING TO MAKE THE PRO CIRCUIT, BUT HE'S
A SMALL MAN IN A LAND OF GIANTS AND NOW
THE BRUTISH DAMAGE CONTROL IS THE LAST
MAN STANDING IN HIS WAY.

IF THERE'S ONE LESSON VON MIDGARD HAS LEARNED IN THE RING, IT'S SIZE ISN'T EVERYTHING.

EVERY WRESTLER AND HIS OPPONENT HAVE THEIR OWN STRENGTHS AND WEAKNESSES.

BY MAXIMIZING HIS OWN STRENGTHS AND FOCUSING THEM ON DAMAGE CONTROL'S WEAKNESSES, VON MIDGARD JUST MAY MAKE IT OUT OF THE RING ALIVE!

AVOID WHAT IS STRONG AND STRIKE AT WHAT IS WEAK.

IF EVER THERE WAS A DAVID AND GOLIATH MATCH-UP, FANS, THIS IS IT!

HIGH-FLYING ERIC VON MIDGARD SQUARES OFF AGANST THE POWERHOUSE, DAMAGE CONTROL!

STRENGTH IS NOT NEARLY AS RELEVANT AS WHERE YOU CONCENTRATE YOUR POWER.

VON MIDGARD KNOWS THAT DAMAGE CONTROL INJURED HIS LEG IN A MATCH THREE WEEKS AGO...

...AND HE'S USING THAT TO SLOW THE BIG MAN DOWN!

KRAK

OPERATING FROM A POWERFUL BASE OF SUPERIORITY IS ESSENTIAL TO WINNING.

SET UP THE FIELD SO YOU CAN BEST APPLY YOUR STRENGTH AGAINST THE ENEMY'S WEAKNESS.

AND NOW VON MIDGARD TAKES TO THE AIR!

KANSAS CITY

2007

OFFICE POLITICS IS NOT OFTEN THOUGHT OF AS WARFARE, BUT IT OFTEN CARRIES ITS OWN VERSION OF CONFLICT AND RESOLUTION. THE STAKES MAY NOT BE AS HIGH PHYSICALLY, BUT THERE IS A LOT RIDING ON THE DECISIONS AND ACTIONS OF THE EMPLOYEES.

SAVVY STAFFERS KNOW WHERE AND WHEN TO FIGHT THEIR BATTLES.

SPEAKING UP AT THE WRONG TIME CAN TURN THEIR CO-WORKERS AGAINST THEM, AND COST THEM GREAT OPPORTUNITIES.

FURTHERMORE, BY PLACING HERSELF IN THE RIGHT POSITION AND REMAINING VIGILANT, EVEN A ROOKIE SECRETARY CAN PUT HERSELF IN THE GOOD GRACES OF HER BOSS.

GET THE ADVANTAGE OF THE GROUND.

EVERY PIECE OF COMPANY CORRESPONDENCE COMES ACROSS THIS DESK. I NEVER PAID MUCH ATTENTION TO IT, SO I WOULDN'T WORRY TOO MUCH ABOUT IT IF I WERE YOU.

WHICH MEANS NOT ONLY SECURING GOOD POSITIONS, BUT AVAILING ONESELF OF NATURAL ADVANTAGES IN EVERY POSSIBLE WAY.

GOOD LUCK!

WELL THIS DOESN'T LOOK RIGHT...

EXCUSE ME MR. DUNCAN. IT MAY BE NOTHING, BUT THERE SEEMS TO BE A DISCREPANCY WITH THESE NUMBERS.

YOU CAN BE SUCCESSFUL OFFENSIVELY ONE HUNDRED TIMES, BUT YOU HAVE TO LOSE ONLY ONCE IN DEFENSE TO LOSE THE BATTLE.

WHY, YOU'RE ABSOLUTELY RIGHT! YOU JUST PREVENTED A POTENTIALLY EMBARRASSING SITUATION FOR ME AND THE COMPANY.

THIS WAS ABOVE AND BEYOND FOR SOMEONE JUST STARTING WITH THE COMPANY. I THINK YOU'LL GO FAR HERE.

MEXICO CITY
1964

THE VIOLENT DRUG CARTELS DEFEND THEIR
BUSINESS FEROCIOUSLY, AND GOING AT
THEM HEAD-ON IS NOT A VIABLE OPTION FOR
OUTGUNNED LAW ENFORCEMENT AGENCIES.
INSTEAD, LAW ENFORCEMENT TURNS TO
UNDERCOVER OPERATIONS.

INFORMATION IS POWER IN THESE OPERATIONS. THE MORE THEY KNOW ABOUT THE CARTEL'S OPERATIONS, THE BETTER PREPARED THEY CAN BE TO STRIKE.

THIS INFORMATION DOES NOT COME TO THEM OVERNIGHT. THE AGENTS MUST BE PATIENT, FLEXIBLE.

AND WHEN THEY STRIKE, THEY MUST REMAIN ON ALERT UNTIL THE CARTELS REACT.

KNOWLEDGE OF THE ENEMY'S DISPOSITIONS CAN ONLY BE OBTAINED FROM OTHER MEN.

THIS IS MY BUDDY, CARL. WE'VE DONE WORK TOGETHER IN THE PAST. HE'S GONNA BE A REAL ASSET FOR US.

INFORMATION IS POWER.

YEAH...SO, IT SOUNDS LIKE WE'RE GONNA BE SELLING THIS BATCH OF GUNS TO SOME HEAVY HITTERS OUT OF MIAMI...

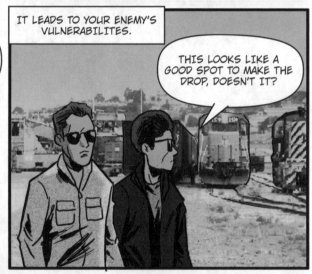

IT LEADS TO YOUR ENEMY'S VULNERABILITES.

THIS LOOKS LIKE A GOOD SPOT TO MAKE THE DROP, DOESN'T IT?

SO, WE'VE BEEN UNDERCOVER NOW FOR CLOSE TO A MONTH. I THINK WE HAVE EVERYTHING WE NEED TO MAKE THE BUST.

THE MORE SPIES YOU HAVE, THE MORE OPPORTUNITIES YOU HAVE TO FURTHER YOUR KNOWLEDGE OF YOUR ENEMY.

ON THE GROUND!

FREEZE!

HANDS BEHIND YOUR HEAD!

IF THERE IS AN OUTBREAK OF FIRE, BUT THE ENEMY'S SOLDIERS REMAIN QUIET, BIDE YOUR TIME AND DO NOT ATTACK.

LOOKS LIKE THE COAST IS CLEAR...

FOCUS ON PATIENCE AND FLEXIBILITY.

TIME TO MAKE A BREAK FOR IT!

SOME ENEMIES WILL NOT RISE TO ANGER QUICKLY.

TO PROTECT THEIR EGO, THEY WILL RESPOND EVENTUALLY.

ALL UNITS! ALL UNITS! THEY'RE TRYING TO MAKE A BREAK OUT THE BACK!

REMAIN ON ALERT UNTIL HE DECIDES TO ACT.

FREEZE!

SAN FRANCISCO 2000

KATE LAWSON JUST GRADUATED COLLEGE AND HAS LANDED A GREAT NEW JOB AND A GORGEOUS APARTMENT OVERLOOKING THE SAN FRANCISCO BAY. SHE AND A FRIEND LOVE TO FREQUENT THE AREA HOT SPOTS AT NIGHT, BUT SHE DOESN'T YET KNOW ALL THE NEIGHBORHOODS A YOUNG WOMAN SHOULD AVOID.

SHE LEARNS THIS LESSON
THE HARD WAY WHEN A CREEP
APPROACHES HER AT THE CLUB,
AND HIS GANG OF THUGS ARE
NOT FAR BEHIND.

BUT KATE'S NO WEAKLING, AND BY BEING UNPREDICTABLE AND
STRIKING HARD AND FAST, SHE KNOWS SHE CAN SAVE HERSELF.

WHEN THE ODDS
ARE AGAINST
HER, SHE KNOWS
RUNNING IS THE
BEST OPTION.

THE SKILLFUL FIGHTER PUTS HERSELF INTO A POSITION WHICH MAKES DEFEAT IMPOSSIBLE.

PERFECT PREY!

LOOK AT THAT CREEP OVER THERE! HE KEEPS ON STARRING AT US. I THINK I'D RATHER GO HOME!

HEY...WANT SOME COMPANY?

UH...SURE. I WAS JUST HEADING TO THE LADIES ROOM, BUT I'LL BE RIGHT BACK

IF YOU ARE UNPREDICTABLE, YOU ARE MOST LIKELY TO SUCCEED.

REACT WISE! IN STILLNESS, YOU ARE MOST VULNERABLE.

I HOPE THE CREEP DOESN`T FOLLOW ME!

WHERE'D SHE GO?

SPLIT UP AND FIND HER!

WHAT!? A *GANG* OF CREEPS? I GOTTA GET OUT OF HERE!

TO SECURE OURSELVES AGAINST DEFEAT LIES IN OUR OWN HANDS, BUT THE OPPORTUNITY OF DEFEATING THE ENEMY IS PROVIDED BY THE ENEMY HIMSELF.

OH NO! WRONG TURN!

GOTCHA!

HE'S DRUNK THAT'S MY CHANCE!

WHEN OPPORTUNITIES TO DECISIVELY DEFEAT YOUR OPPONENT ARISE, TAKE IMMEDIATE ACTION.

UGH!

LUCKY DADDY TAUGHT ME SOME KARATE! BUT THIS WON'T HELP ME NOW!

THERE SHE IS!

CONVERSELY, WHEN YOU BECOME AWARE OF THE IMPOSSIBILITY OF A WINNING OUTCOME, IMMEDIATELY WITHDRAW.

RUN! SISTER.

VANCOUVER
2005

RON THORNDALE HAS JUST PUSHED A
MAJOR PRODUCT THROUGH R&D, BUT NOW
THINGS ARE GETTING BOGGED DOWN IN THE
MARKETING DEPARTMENT. EVERY LITTLE
DECISION IS GOING THROUGH A COMMITTEE,
AND THE DELAYS ARE PUTTING HIS WHOLE
PROJECT IN JEOPARDY.

TIRED OF WAITING, HE BRINGS IN JULIUS WELLS, A NEW RECRUIT MORE CONCERNED WITH THE COMPANY'S SUCCESS THAN MAKING THE FEW PEOPLE ON HIS TEAM HAPPY.

JULIUS UNDERSTANDS THE VALUE OF SPEED AND THE COSTS OF DELAYS. HE GOES WITH HIS GUT AND IS UNAFRAID TO MAKE DECISIONS.

SUBSEQUENT DECISIONS BECOME EVEN EASIER, AND PRETTY SOON THE TEAM HAS REAL MOMENTUM ON THEIR SIDE.

CLEVERNESS HAS NEVER BEEN ASSOCIATED WITH LONG DELAYS.

GREAT WORK, EVERYONE!

NOW LET'S GET THIS NEW PROJECT TO MARKET!

SPEED IS INVALUABLE.

I'M NOT SURE ABOUT THE COLOR SCHEME...

YOU CAN GAIN THE ADVANTAGE BY MAKING ADJUSTMENTS ON THE BATTLEFIELD MORE QUICKLY THAN YOUR ADVERSARY.

SO, THE GOAL OF THIS FOCUS GROUP IS TO ADDRESS THE COLOR SCHEME FOR OUR NEW WEB OFFERING...

CAN WE ALSO TALK ABOUT THE LOGO DESIGN?

ONE CAN BEAT A MORE INTELLIGENT PERSON BY SHEER FORCE OF RAPIDITY.

I JUST HEARD FROM OUR TOP CLIENT THAT MALCO IS PUTTING TOGETHER A SIMILAR PRODUCT...

DELAY IS THE ENEMY.

WE'VE BEEN DRAGGING OUR FEET, AND NOW OUR BIGGEST COMPETITOR IS CLOSE TO OFFERING A SIMILAR PRODUCT! WE'VE GOT TO BUILD SOME MOMENTUM!

WHILE STRATEGIC DECISIONS REQUIRE DELIBERATE THINKING, TACTICAL DECISIONS MUST BE MADE THROUGH GUT REACTION AND INSTINCT.

IN EVERYTHING WE DO, OPPORTUNITIES MAKE THEMSELVES AVAILABLE QUICKLY AND THEN RETREAT JUST AS QUICKLY.

I'M PUTTING JULIUS IN CHARGE OF GETTING THIS PROJECT FINISHED.

WITH ALL GREAT STRATEGISTS, FROM JULIUS CAESAR TO NAPOLEON, THE VALUE OF TIME-THAT IS, BEING A LITTLE AHEAD OF YOUR OPPONENT-HAS COUNTED FOR MORE THAN EITHER NUMERICAL SUPERIORITY OR THE NICEST CALCULATIONS.

THE TEAM NEDDS ANOTHER COUPLE OF WEEKS TO DISCUSS THE COLOR...

WE'RE GOING WITH THE BLUE.

BY COMBINING SPEED WITH CONCENTRATION (STRIKING WEAKNESS) WE CREATE MOMENTUM.

WE DID IT!

THE END

ABOUT THE AUTHOR

The legend goes that *Sun Tzu* was born into minor nobility in what is now Shandong, a part of China north of Shanghai. Born "Sun Wu," he was given a good education and wrote a military treatise in order to get noticed and hired by royalty. Sun Tzu expanded his 13-chapter Art of War into 82 chapters and trained the army. Eventually he broke the peace by invading the southern state of Yue. Other conflicts ensued but although his troops were once outnumbered 30,000 to 200,000 he was always victorious. Many successes followed and continued after his death. Some considered his death to be another of his deceptions.

ABOUT THE ARTIST

At six years old, *Shane Clester* realized that most people aren't happy with their jobs. Even as he drew robots just to see if he could, he decided at that young age that he would turn his artistic play into work. As Shane grew older and studied the nuances of art, his initial excitement evolved into fascination.

He was compelled by the replication of life through seemingly limited tools, and embarked on a quest to learn technical proficiency. In the early 2000s, Shane studied briefly under Jim Garrison, well-known for his art anatomy and technical skills.

Shane then relocated from Arizona to California, where he learned a powerful lesson: You have to study to be an artist, and then you have to learn the business of being an artist.

QUIZ

Q.1 The very first thing you must do before you go into battle is:

A. Analyze your enemy.

B. Count the cost.

C. Prepare your army.

Q.2 If you have to go to war, the aim is to:

A. Win quickly and with minimal loss.

B. Win quickly at any cost.

C. Win at any cost.

Q.3 Going to war without strategy:

A. Can only be compensated for with smart tactics.

B. Makes success a mere gamble.

C. Invokes the best in us.

Q.4 A weaker army can defeat a stronger army through:

A. Formlessness and speed

B. Strong defense

C. Strong offense

Q.5 A superior number of soldiers does not always equal a greater advantage because:

A. How you utilize your resources best determines advantage.

B. How fast you move best determines advantage.

C. How well you defend best determines advantage.

Q.6 You can beat a much stronger enemy by:

A. Focusing your weakness against the enemy's weakness.

B. Focusing your strength against the enemy's strength.

C. Focusing your strength against the enemy's weakness.

Q.7 If you're in battle and you become aware that you cannot win, you should:

A. Withdraw immediately.

B. Continue to battle.

C. Divide your army.

Q.8 You can beat a more intelligent enemy by:

A.. Prolonging the battle

B.. Sheer force of rapidity

C. Changing your strategy.

Q.9 If you are unpredictable, you are most likely to:

A. Fail

B. Succeed

C. Retreat

Q.10 The height of wisdom for a general is to:

A. Win as quickly as possible.

B. Win at any price.

C. Win without a battle.

Answers on the next page.

QUIZ ANSWERS

1 (A) Analyze your enemy.

2 (A) Win quickly and with minimal loss.

3 (B) Makes success a mere gamble.

4 (A) Formlessness and speed.

5 (A) How you utilize your resources best determines advantage.

6 (C) Focusing your strength against the enemy's weakness.

7 (A) Withdraw immediately.

8 (B) Sheer force of rapidity.

9 (B) Succeed.

10 (C) Win without a battle.

"ABSORB THE SECRET OF WINNING ANY BATTLE" AS AN MP3 WITHOUT OPENING YOUR EYES.

To get access to the studio-created audio book, please go to the following website: www.smartercomics.com/audiobooks

Your code is: 2500

Other titles from
Smarter**Comics**®

The 50th Law
from SmarterComics

by 50 Cent and Robert Greene

Focus your hustler's eye on this comic book adaptation of my secret to success. Find out how I went from the hard life in Queens to the top of the music charts -- and the business world.

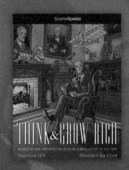

THINK & GROW RICH
from SmarterComics

by Napoleon Hill

Want to learn the principles of getting rich in less than an hour? Take the illustrated advice of millionaire Andrew Carnegie, whose observations make up the heart of the best-selling classic "Think and Grow Rich." Now updated into an engaging comic book format, you can quickly glean Carnegie's wisdom from these beautifully illustrated panels.

The Book of 5 Rings
from SmarterComics

by Miyamoto Musashi

Infamous 17th century samurai Miyamoto Musashi (1584-1645) never lost a fight. His unprecedented winning streak wasn't based on supernatural powers: he was a keen master of strategy, timing, and the nuances of human interaction. He recorded his brilliant observations in „The Book of Five Rings" in 1643.

Eat that Frog!
from SmarterComics

by Brian Tracy

Success is not a magical com-bination of genetics and fashion sense. Rather, it is a series of time management behaviors which must be practiced on a regular basis. Luckily, "EAT THAT FROG!" will show you how to deal with those challenging tasks you keep putting off in an accessible comic book format.

Other titles from
SmarterComics®

Financial Intelligence
from SmarterComics

by Karen Berman & Joe Knight

Want to know what accounting numbers really mean without flatlining your pulse? Ditch the dry numbers and check out this comic book version!

Fortune Favors the Bold
from SmarterComics

by Franco Arda

Written by the founder of SmarterComics, this powerful little manual packs a punch. If you want to grab life by the horns but tend to drag your feet doing it, this comic is for you.

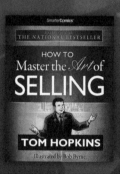

How to Master the Art of Selling
from SmarterComics

by Tom Hopkins

A national bestseller, with over one million copies sold in its original version, this book is a classic for teaching the tools of selling success. Lauded by motivational icon Zig Ziglar, the author has been called "America's #1 sales trainer."

The 80/20 Principle
from SmarterComics

by Richard Koch

Learn the time-tested secret of achieving more with less using "the 80/20 Principle." Based on the counter-intuitive fact that 80% of results flow from 20% of causes, it is the guiding principle of highly effective people and organizations.

www.SMARTERCOMICS.com

SmarterComics is a visionary publishing company based in California's Silicon Valley. Combining time-tested texts with vivid 21st century illustration and display techniques, SmarterComics bridges the gap between the old and new publishing models.

Our award-winning illustrators refined their chops at prestigious companies including Marvel and DC Comics. Our script writer and editor won the Eisner and the Harvey Awards, the comic genre's equivalent of the Oscars. SmarterComics itself has been named by Entrepreneur Magazine as one of their "100 Brilliant Companies."

Basically, we're awesome.